Volcanoes

Louise Spencely

OXFORD
UNIVERSITY PRESS

Contents

What is a volcano?

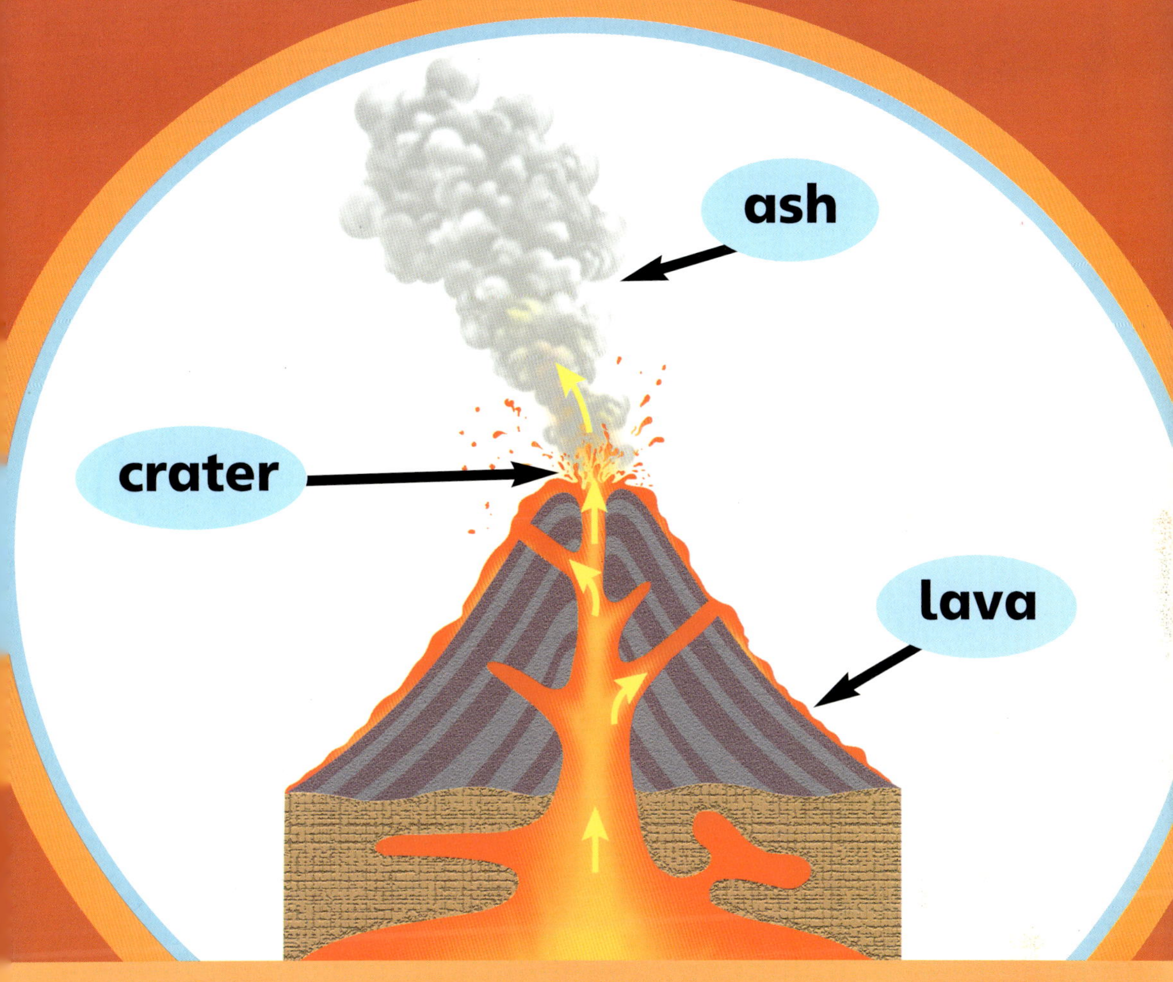

A volcano is a mountain with a hole in the top. The hole is called a crater. Underneath, deep down inside the Earth, there is hot, melted rock. It can bubble up into the crater.

Eruption!

Sometimes a volcano blows up.
This is called an eruption.

The melted rock boils and bubbles.
Hot ash is thrown into the sky.

The melted rock boils over and runs down the sides of the volcano. It is called lava. Sometimes the lava runs into the sea. It makes the sea boil.

The ash is blown away. It can travel a long way from the volcano.

After the eruption

The lava cools down and stops moving. When it gets cold, it turns into rock.

The new rock makes the land around the volcano look very different.

Volcanoes in the news

When a volcano erupts it is very dangerous. People living near it have to leave their homes.

Everything is covered in lava and ash. Sometimes, their homes are burnt or buried.

When a volcano erupts, there may be pictures of it in the newspapers.

People hurry away from the danger.

Volcanoes and nature

A lot of trees and plants die when a volcano erupts. Animals run away. Birds fly off to a safer place.

Soon the trees and plants grow again. Animals and birds will come back soon.

The ash turns into very rich soil.
It helps plants to grow well.
So there is lots of good food for people and animals.

Some very old lava has gold or silver in it. People dig it out and sell it.

Types of volcano

Some volcanoes are active.

They are erupting now, or they have erupted just a few years ago.

Some volcanoes are sleeping. They are called dormant volcanoes.

This dormant volcano has not erupted for thousands of years.

Some very old volcanoes will
never erupt again.

This old volcano is extinct. It will never erupt again.

They are called extinct volcanoes.

Index